It's a
GOD
Thing!

To:

....

From:

....

Written by Karen Hill

Illustrated by Dan Brawner

Thomas Nelson, Inc.
Nashville

Library of Congress Control Number: 00–135736

ISBN 0-8499-7601-4 (Pink)
ISBN 0-8499-7602-2 (Green)

Printed in China

01 02 03 04 05 PPI 9 8 7 6 5 4 3 2 1

With love to the
Oak Hills Church of Christ Youth Group.

Special thanks to Caroline Green,
Andrea Lucado, Hayley Pickens,
Noel Whiteside, and Kara Wilson.

". . . you shine like
stars in the universe. . . ."

Philippians 2:15 (NIV)

What's Inside

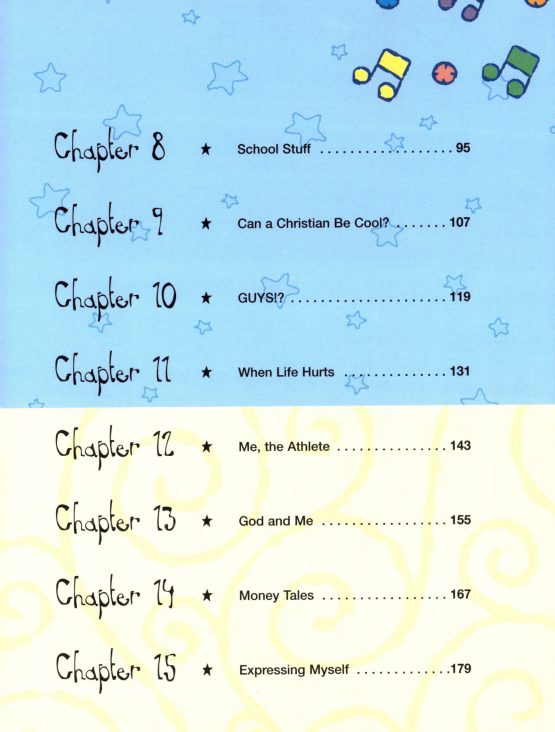

Introduction

Hey, Girl!

My name's Karen, and I wrote this book because I think girls are awesome! And because I know girls have tons of great stuff to say! Now, I have to confess: I'm a LOT older than you, but I haven't forgotten what it's like to be a *tweenager*—I remember feeling stuck between being a kid and being a grownup. Besides, I have two girls of my own. And I work on youth projects with middle-school-age girls at my church. Best of all, I had a team of girls your age who helped me plan this book, so I'd know what you would want to write about in this journal. I think they came up with some super ideas, and they even shared some of their own experiences. I hope you'll enjoy getting to know my "buds" as you make your way through *It's a God Thing!*

Speaking of *It's a God Thing!* let's talk about this title for a minute. Have you heard the expression before? It's kind of a new one, but it's starting to catch on. A "God Thing" is something powerful that happens to you or someone you know. It's not magic or mystery, it's God being active in your life. It's the kind of thing that you couldn't possibly have done on your own, or it's a humongous blessing, or . . . well, a great example of this is in the chapter about friendship. Read what *my* friend Kara has to say about a "God Thing" that happened in her life.

We've included fifteen chapters, which I hope will cover the many pieces of your life. Since you have *so* much to say, there are plenty of journaling pages at the end of each section. This is not a day-to-day diary—it's a journal for any day: the days when you're feeling creative ("Expressing Myself"), or when you wonder how to deal with difficult times ("Tough Stuff"), or those confusing days when you just have to write about guys ("Guys!?").

Share your heart on the pages of this book—it's yours. It's a safe place to go when life gets weird or when life is great.

I pray this book will be fun and inspiring for you—it's been both of those things for me. In fact, writing *It's a God Thing!* has been a God Thing in my life.

Your friend,

Karen Hill

all about me

Chapter 1

Paste a favorite photo of yourself right here.

"Is there someone who worships the Lord? The Lord will point him to the best way. He will enjoy a good life." **Psalm 25:12–13**

11

Me, Myself, and I . . .

"e" is a tiny word for who I really am.

There's a lot more to me than what the world sees.

Sure, there are millions of girls my age, and some of us even

look alike. But there's just one me. I have dreams galore and

plans for my life.

I'm just me and that's great. I can be serious or I can

be silly. I can be caring, but sometimes I'm hurtful. Usually I

do what's right, but sometimes I don't. I like having fun with

friends, but sometimes I enjoy being by myself.

Some days I feel grown-up; other days I act like a kid.

Guess you'd say, "I'm a girl!"

My full name:_____

Where I was born: _____

When I was born: _____

I weighed _____

It's a God Thing!

The "Me" Basket

There's a basket called "me" and here's what's inside . . .

Bundles of dreams

Bits of schemes

A few tiny tears

One or two fears

Giggles and grins

Losses and wins

Friends and fads

Good times and bad

Homework and malls

And lots of phone calls!

In a nutshell, here's the story of me:

My nickname is

_____

These are the people who use
my nickname:

_____

_____

_____

_____

My world is made up of these
people and pets:

_____

_____

_____

_____

_____

This is a list of my favorite things
to do alone:

_____

_____

_____

_____

_____

_____

These are the things I hate to do:

_____

_____

_____

_____

_____

_____

If I had a free afternoon, I'd spend it

_____

_____

_____

_____

_____

_____

_____

_____

_____

If I could go anywhere in the
whole world, I'd go to

_____

_____

It's a God Thing!

Once there, I would like to

_____
_____
_____
_____
_____
_____
_____
_____
_____

I get energized about

_____
_____
_____
_____
_____
_____

_____
_____
_____

I'm really determined about

_____
_____
_____
_____
_____
_____
_____
_____
_____
_____
_____
_____
_____
_____

"In all you do, give thanks to God the Father through Jesus."

Colossians 3:17

all about me

Think Ahead

Our youth minister was talking about peer pressure and how to deal with typical teen situations—like drugs, or getting involved in sex, or being in a group of kids who want to steal. One thing he asked hit me like a ton of bricks: "How will you know how to handle these situations, if you don't think about them ahead of time?" He said we should imagine ourselves in each situation and decide what we'll do and say ahead of time. "You need to know right now whether you'll say yes or no, because in the heat of the moment you may not be able to make a wise choice."

I did as he suggested. After I thought through some of the tricky situations that might come up, I also thought about what kind of person I wanted to be. I decided to make a contract with myself—a promise that I intend to keep.

Contract with Myself

Karen's Contract:

Each day, for the rest of my life, I promise to
Pray,
Listen,
Encourage someone,
Keep myself sexually pure,
Find something to love in everyone,
Think before I speak or act,
Respect others,
Keep the Ten Commandments,
Be a friend,
Seek forgiveness, and
Do everything I can to make God proud of me.

Write Your Own Contract:

_____
_____
_____
_____
_____
_____
_____
_____
_____
_____
_____
_____

Music

My favorite style of music is

....

What I like about it is

....

....

....

I always listen to this singer (group):

....

The music makes me feel

....

....

Sometimes, I think the song ....
was written just for me because (tell why)

....

....

....

....

If I wrote a song about my life, I'd use words like

....

....

....

Dreams

I have so many dreams for my life. Here are my hopes and dreams:

....

....

....

....

....

....

....

....

....

....

....

....

....

....

....

....

....

....

....

....

....

....

....

....

Goals

In five years, I hope I'll be doing this:

....
....
....
....
....
....
....
....
....
....
....
....

In five years, I hope I have accomplished these goals:

....
....
....
....
....
....
....
....
....
....
....

It's a God Thing!

In ten years, I hope I'll be doing this:

....
....
....
....
....
....
....
....
....
....
....

In ten years, I hope I have accomplished these goals:

....
....
....
....
....
....
....
....
....
....
....

A GOD THING MOMENT IN MY LIFE

(On this page, write about a God Thing that has happened to you.)

....

....

....

....

....

....

....

....

....

....

....

....

....

....

....

....

....

....

....

....

....

....

....

....

....

The Family Factor

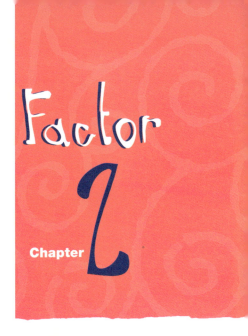

Chapter 2

After filling in the blanks, create a design around your family history.
Add more lines, if you need them.

My Family and Me:

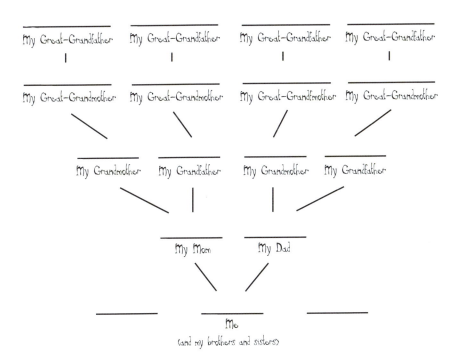

My Great-Grandfather

My Great-Grandfather

My Great-Grandfather

My Great-Grandfather

My Great-Grandmother

My Great-Grandmother

My Great-Grandmother

My Great-Grandmother

My Grandmother

My Grandfather

My Grandmother

My Grandfather

My Mom

My Dad

Me
(and my brothers and sisters)

Family Forever . . .

Have you ever watched the clouds in the sky? Floating, changing shape as they drift by. Tiny wispy clouds, huge puffy clouds—all shapes and sizes. You can almost see a familiar face, if you look long enough. A family is something like a sky full of clouds—all shapes, sizes, sometimes moving in different directions. Even though the members of a family aren't all alike, a family can be a beautiful place where good memories are made.

Below are the people in my family and what makes each one special.

Name	His/Her "Specialness"
_____	_____
_____	_____
_____	_____
_____	_____
_____	_____
_____	_____
_____	_____

It's a God Thing!

What Girls Say about Families:

"I'm never lonely, but I hate sharing the bathroom!"
—Martha, 14

"Sometimes it's hard to accept that my parents know what's best for me."
—Dawn, 12

"I'm the youngest in the family, and sometimes that makes me feel alone."
—Kristen, 13

"The best thing about having an older sister is she can drive me places!"
—Kasey, 13

"I wish my parents would give me more freedom."
—Morgan, 14

"My little sister always thinks she's right, but I want her to listen to me and do what I tell her. After all, I'm older!"
—Caroline, 15

"I have a great relationship with my parents. They always give me the answers I'm looking for."
—Anna, 12

"My sisters and brothers are embarrassing and weird. But I love them anyway. Who can figure that out?"
—Lauren, 13

Here's what I say about my family:

"_____

_____

_____

_____

_____"

My Family

Our favorite activity as a family is

_____

_____

_____

_____

_____

_____

My family is unique because

_____

_____

_____

_____

_____

_____

_____

_____

_____

_____

_____

_____

_____

_____

_____

The funniest person in my family is

_____

because_____

_____

_____

_____

_____

If I could change one thing about my family, it would be

_____

_____

_____

_____

_____

It's a God Thing!

My Mom Always Says:

"Be a leader, not a follower."
—Noel, 14

"A face without freckles is like a sky without stars."
—Lee, 14

"Can't never could do anything."
—Kathy, 14

My Dad Always Says:

"Stand up straight."
—Carol, 15

"Eat your carrots and you'll have rosy cheeks."
—Madison, 12

"Rise and shine, Sunshine!"
—Dawn, 13

Add your mom's favorite sayings here:

"_____
_____
_____"

Add your dad's favorite sayings here:

"_____
_____
_____"

The "Gone" Game

In all families, problems are bound to appear, just like rain clouds on a sunny day. They weren't planned or expected, but they come along anyway. When it seems hard to get along or work through a difficulty, play the "Gone Game." Imagine a world in which you have no family—they're all gone; you're all alone. When you play the Gone Game, you'll begin to see how much you need and love your family, even with its problems. God can help you work through it. He can help you love them more than before. Just ask him!

Here's a family situation I'm praying about:

_____
_____
_____
_____

Learning to Forgive

We had a substitute teacher in English. Before the dismissal bell rang, she said, "Well, that's all, folks." The class thought she meant the period was over, so everyone started to leave. She followed us out into the hall and started yelling at us to get back into the room. Next thing we knew, about twenty of us were in the principal's office! I couldn't believe it when Mr. Hughes handed each of us a discipline report to take home. It was totally humiliating! I wanted to cry like everything, but somehow I managed to wait until I got home.

All afternoon I dreaded telling my parents. Would they be disappointed in me? Ashamed? What would they say? I was a nervous wreck! But when I showed my mom the report (the principal had marked "showed disrespect for teacher"), my mom just hugged me, saying, "This must be a mistake. I don't know the teacher, but I know *you*." Wow! What an awesome moment!

My mom was incredible—she talked to me about forgiving others, even when their mistakes hurt us. Then we prayed about it. The next day, the sub was back again. She started the class by saying, "You know, I want to apologize for yesterday. I think the whole thing was a big misunderstanding, and I'm sorry I overreacted."

In that moment, God helped me see that you're never too old to make mistakes, and you're never too young to forgive. I couldn't wait to get home and tell my mom!

—Lindsey

Family

Here's what "Family Forever" means to me:

....
....
....
....
....
....
....
....
....
....
....
....
....
....
....
....
....
....
....
....
....
....
....
....
....
....

Memories

Some of my favorite family memories:

....
....
....
....
....
....
....
....
....
....
....
....
....
....
....
....
....
....
....
....
....
....
....
....
....
....
....
....

Best Time

Our best time together as a family was when:

....
....
....
....
....
....
....
....
....
....
....
....
....
....
....
....
....
....
....
....
....
....
....
....
....
....
....

Our House

Living together sometimes creates chaos. Here's a story about a crazy time at my house:

....
....
....
....
....
....
....
....
....
....
....
....
....
....
....
....
....
....
....
....
....
....
....
....
....
....

Relatives

Every family has its share of unusual relatives. Here are mine:

....
....
....
....
....
....
....
....
....
....
....
....
....
....
....
....
....
....
....
....
....
....
....
....
....
....
....
....
....
....
....

A GOD THING MOMENT
WITH MY FAMILY

(On this page, write about a God Thing that has happened to you and your family.)

....

....

....

....

....

....

....

....

....

....

....

....

....

....

....

....

....

....

....

....

....

....

....

....

....

A Day in the Life of Me . . .

Chapter 3

Write your own headline—something special about your day.

MY DAY . . .

*B*egins when the maid brings a breakfast tray to my four-poster bed on the third floor of my fifty-room mansion. "Butter my croissant for me," I tell her, as I decide which of my three thousand matching outfits I'll wear today. "Tell the chauffeur to have the limo ready at eight sharp," I remind her. Ah, life is wonderful—huh? What? Time to catch the bus? Bummer! Just when my dream was getting interesting!

Here's a typical day in my life:

7 A.M. _____

8 A.M. _____

9 A.M. _____

10 A.M. _____

11 A.M. _____

noon _____

1 P.M. _____

2 P.M. _____

3 P.M. _____

4 P.M. _____

5 P.M. _____

6 P.M. _____

7 P.M. _____

8 P.M. _____

9 P.M. _____

10 P.M. _____

It's a God Thing!

Today's Checklist:

"But the Spirit gives love, joy, peace, patience, kindness, goodness, faithfulness, gentleness, self-control."

Galatians 5:22

Today I'll work on at least one "fruit of the Spirit":

_____ **love**

_____ **joy**

_____ **peace**

_____ **patience**

_____ **kindness**

_____ **goodness**

_____ **faithfulness**

_____ **gentleness**

_____ **self-control**

___ Spend time alone with God

___ Exercise

___ Do something nice for someone else

___ Chores: _____

_____

_____

_____

_____

___ Go to _____

___ Call _____

_____

_____

___ Do these things:

_____

_____

_____

_____

_____

_____

_____

_____

_____

Good Morning, Girl!

Alarm rings. Feet hit cold floor. Water splashes on face. Eyes begin to open. Who's that in the mirror? Brown hair, brown eyes, rosy cheeks. I see a girl, about five feet, five inches, in an over-sized T-shirt, boxers too small, and floppy Eeyore slippers. She yawns at me, braces glimmering in the light. *Hmmm*, she thinks as the sweet smell of waffles drifts up the stairs. "Hello day, here I come!"

—Jennifer

"Plan ahead . . . it wasn't raining when Noah built the ark."

Anonymous

The best part of my day is

_____
_____
_____
_____
_____
_____
_____

The hardest part of my day is

_____
_____
_____
_____
_____
_____
_____
_____
_____

Most days, I like to think about

_____
_____
_____
_____
_____
_____
_____

It's a God Thing!

Make Each Day Count!

You can never recapture yesterday. Or even the hour before this one. Time runs away like a helium balloon floating off into the distant sky. So make each day count. Turn bad days around—don't just veg out, pouting about what happened or didn't happen today. Find something good in each day. Just keep looking; it's there! Find a reason to remember this day because each day is a gift from God.

Something good about today:

_____

_____

_____

Fitting everything into my daily

schedule is crazy! I'm praying

about these activities and asking

for God's help in organizing my day:

_____

_____

_____

_____

IT'S A GOD THING!

Bad Day, Good Day

The day started out to be the worst day of my life. My parents had left on a week-long trip, and they had divided up all of us kids among various friends (there are five kids in our family). I had fun staying at my friend's house for the first couple of days, but then I got a bad case of homesickness. I really missed my family, and it felt like forever before we'd all be back together again. I didn't even think about the times we didn't get along and having to share and all that—I just thought about missing them. I prayed about it and told God just how I felt.

That afternoon, I went to my house to feed my dog. It felt sad, being there in my empty house — it was never this quiet! Just about then I heard a knock at the front door. My older brother and sister had come by to see me! The bad day turned good when I saw their faces (they even let me hug them!). It was a great God moment!

—Erika

Today

These are my priorities today:

....

....

....

....

....

....

....

....

....

....

....

....

....

....

....

....

....

....

....

....

....

....

....

....

....

....

....

....

Minutes to Hours

If I could make a day as long as I wanted, here's what I'd do with
the extra time:

....
....
....
....
....
....
....
....
....
....
....
....
....
....
....
....
....
....
....
....
....
....
....
....
....
....
....

It's a God Thing!

If I could design the perfect day, it would be like this:
I would go

....
....
....
....
....
....
....
....

I would talk to

....
....
....
....
....
....

I would do these things:

....
....
....
....
....
....
....
....

Life

I'm going to get better organized at

....
....
....
....
....
....
....
....
....
....
....
....
....
....
....
....
....
....
....
....
....
....
....
....
....
....

It's a God Thing!

Imagine you are forty. Now, write a letter to your best friend about what your day is like when you are forty.

....
....
....
....
....
....
....
....
....
....
....
....
....
....
....
....
....
....
....
....
....
....
....
....
....
....
....
....
....
....
....
....

A GOD THING MOMENT IN MY DAILY LIFE

(On this page, write about a God Thing that has happened to you.)

....

....

....

....

....

....

....

....

....

....

....

....

....

....

....

....

....

....

....

....

....

....

....

....

Will the Real Me Please Stand Up?

Chapter 4

On this page, trace several keys. Then write words in the keys that describe the *real* you.

"God does not see the same way people see. People look at the outside of a person, but the Lord looks at the heart." **1 Samuel 16:7**

When You Look in the Mirror . . .

What do you see? What do you want to see? What do you think others see? But, most important, what does God see? Whether you like what's in the mirror or see room for improvement, remember what God sees in you! He doesn't see a beautiful face or a parade of zits. He doesn't see scars or fat or gorgeous hair. He sees your heart. Look in the mirror again, and look at yourself as God's creation. Wow! Aren't you a knockout! We are all beautiful when we use God's eyes!

On the outside,
I look like this:

Hair_____

Eyes _____

Height _____

Weight _____

This is what I'm like on the inside:

___Compassionate

___Selfish

___Curious

___Outgoing

___Prayerful

___Giving

___Creative

___Shy

___Loving

___Truthful

___Quiet

___Studious

"Sticks and stones may break your bones, but words can really hurt!"

I was running late for first class. I opened my locker and reached over the guy below me. As my locker door swung open, my mirror fell, hitting Mike's head.

"Ow! Watch it, Fatso!" he yelled.

"I'm sor—" I tried, but he glared at me and walked away.

Fat? Maybe it was my outfit. Or the way I did my hair. *Oh well, can't think about that right now*, I told myself. *Better get to class.*

"Cows go moo-o-o and so do you-o-o!" It was Mike.

Unfortunately, he sat next to me in Spanish. He kept on calling me "fat," "tubby," you name it—until I began to believe him. Everyone else around me started looking skinny, like the girls in magazines and on TV.

For a while, I let Mike's words influence me into forgetting that my body—tall or short, fat or skinny—is God's design. But then I remembered that God made me just the way I am. God loves me, and he's the only one who counts.

—Jennifer

These are the things I like about my appearance:

_____
_____
_____
_____
_____
_____
_____
_____
_____
_____
_____
_____
_____

If I could change something about my appearance, it would be

_____
_____
_____
_____
_____
_____

It's a God Thing!

I'm totally content with my appearance.

____YES   ____NO

I'm trying to improve *my outer self* this way:

_____

_____

_____

_____

_____

_____

_____

_____

_____

_____

_____

_____

_____

_____

IT'S A GOD THING!

Show the World What's Inside

Your attitude determines how others look at you. It doesn't matter how much makeup you wear—if you are sitting in a corner, frowning, no one is going to talk to you. Since I learned this, I have become more content with myself. Sure, on some days I wish my hair wouldn't be as poofy, or the circles under my eyes wouldn't show up as much, but if I have a smile in my heart, it will show on my face. A smile gets more people's attention than ten thousand pounds of makeup!

—Hayley

> "What dominates your thoughts defines you."
> **Karen Hill**

Some people I know whose great attitudes make them beautiful:

_____

_____

_____

_____

_____

_____

_____

_____

Beautiful Me

What makes me beautiful in God's eyes:

....
....
....
....
....
....
....
....
....
....
....
....
....
....
....
....
....
....
....
....
....
....
....
....
....
....
....

Attitude

Times when my attitude has been good:

....
....
....
....
....
....
....
....
....
....
....

Times when I needed an "attitude adjustment":

....
....
....
....
....
....
....
....
....
....
....
....

The Inner Me

This is what I like best about the inner me:

....
....
....
....
....
....
....
....
....
....
....
....
....
....

I'm trying to improve the inner me this way:

....
....
....
....
....
....
....
....
....
....
....

Made by God

These are some things that God expects of me:

....
....
....
....
....
....
....
....
....
....
....
....
....
....
....
....
....
....
....
....
....
....
....
....
....
....

These are some things I need to work on:

....
....
....
....
....
....
....
....
....
....
....
....
....
....
....
....
....
....
....
....
....
....
....
....
....

A GOD THING MOMENT ABOUT MY APPEARANCE

(On this page, write about a God Thing that has happened to you.)

....
....
....
....
....
....
....
....
....
....
....
....
....
....
....
....
....
....
....
....
....
....
....
....
....
....

Welcome Aboard the Friend-Ship!

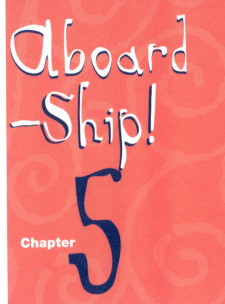

Chapter 5

All aboard! On this page, design your own ship and paste photos of your friends on it.

Friends:
Choosing . . . Keeping . . . Being

efinition: A friend is someone who cares about you, likes you, and is loyal to you, no matter what. It's like this: Imagine you're onstage and it's time for curtain call. If no one in the audience applauds for you, your friend will give you a standing ovation. Even if you sang off-key, even if you bumbled your lines, your friend would still applaud. She knows you didn't sing so great, she knows you messed up, but she's still glad you're her friend.

The story of my best friends:

Friend's Name	Where We Met	What We Do Together
_____	_____	_____
_____	_____	_____
_____	_____	_____
_____	_____	_____
_____	_____	_____
_____	_____	_____
_____	_____	_____
_____	_____	_____

It's a God Thing!

GIRL TALK: My Best Friend . . .

". . . always listens to me and isn't afraid to tell me how she feels."

—Lisa, 15

". . . is so much fun—she's not embarrassed to be silly sometimes."

—Martie, 13

". . . lets me tell her how I feel about life."

—Liz, 14

". . . isn't judgmental, and is very trustworthy."

—Leah, 15

". . . lets me know she appreciates me and doesn't take me for granted."

—Rachel, 12

Best Buds

I like to hang out with

_____

_____

_____

_____

_____

> " . . . good advice from a friend is sweet."
>
> **Proverbs 27:9**

Mostly, we enjoy doing these things together:

_____

_____

_____

_____

_____

Once, something really weird happened when we were together. Here's the story:

_____

_____

_____

_____

_____

_____

_____

_____

_____

_____

I think the most important thing to remember about being a good friend is

_____

_____

_____

_____

_____

It's a God Thing!

Choosing Friends

It was kind of hard for me to choose my group of friends this year. A lot of new cliques were formed and many of my friends changed groups, along with changing personalities to fit in. I think it's important not to change friends just to be popular.

There is one girl at my school who's made fun of by the other students. In sixth grade I never talked to her much because of the way people felt about her. But over the next year, I began to talk to her. I discovered she is a really cool person. Because of her, I've come to realize that who you are means more than what you look like. I consider her a friend, no matter what anyone else thinks.

—Andrea

The qualities I look for in a friend include:

_____
_____
_____
_____
_____
_____
_____
_____
_____
_____
_____
_____
_____

Once, I had to tell a friend I was sorry. This is what happened:

_____
_____
_____
_____
_____
_____
_____
_____
_____
_____
_____
_____
_____

IT'S A GOD THING!

Prayer for a Friend

Seventh grade was a nightmare for me: I didn't have one single friend.

One night I broke down crying and prayed that God would send some-

one to be my friend. A few days later, another girl and I were assigned

to do a project together. She came over to my house to work on the

project, and we began to talk about school and pressure and stuff like

that. She said, "I've been praying so long for a friend, but so far, God

hasn't sent one." I just froze. I told her that I had been praying the same

prayer. We both realized that God was answering our prayers at that

very moment. It was truly a God Thing, and I am truly grateful.

—Kara

Together

So far, the most fun I've had with my friends was when

....
....
....
....
....
....
....
....
....
....
....
....
....
....
....
....
....
....
....
....
....
....
....
....
....
....
....
....
....

Friends

Here's how my friend(s) and I are alike:

....
....
....
....
....
....
....
....
....
....

Here's how my friend(s) and I are different:

....
....
....
....
....
....
....
....
....
....
....
....
....
....
....

Being the new kid in school (or church or the neighborhood) is tough.
I know because

....
....
....
....
....
....
....
....
....
....
....
....
....
....
....
....
....
....
....
....
....
....
....
....
....
....

Sharing

My friend(s) and I don't agree on everything, but we respect each other's views. Something we disagree on is

....

....

....

....

My favorite friend to talk with on the phone is

....

....

....

....

We talk about

....

....

....

....

....

....

....

My favorite friend to play sports with is

....
....
....
....

My favorite friend to confide in is

....
....
....
....

If I had a big problem, I'd call

....
....
....
....
....
....

If I had a funny experience, I'd call

....
....
....
....

If I just wanted to hang out, I'd call

....
....
....
....
....

A GOD THING MOMENT
WITH MY FRIENDS

(On this page, write about a God Thing that has happened to you and your friends.)

....
....
....
....
....
....
....
....
....
....
....
....
....
....
....
....
....
....
....
....
....
....
....
....
....
....
....
....

Tough Stuff

Chapter 6

Circle the words that describe things you've had to deal with:

anger

depression

abuse

unkind remarks

failures

conflict with a teacher, neighbor, or family member

misunderstanding with a friend

criticism

disappointment

What Do I Do with My Problems?

et's face it: There are more than a few bumps and potholes in the road of life. Tough stuff just happens, often when we least expect it. When a difficult time comes into our lives, we can do what we can to make it better, accept it, get totally depressed over it, ask someone for help, or we can pray about it. The main thing is: Instead of letting a tough time rule your life, think about what the best way is to deal with it.

My toughest challenge has been

_____

_____

Here's what I've done to work through it:

_____

_____

_____

_____

It's a God Thing!

The biggest mistake I've made is

_____

_____

_____

_____

_____

_____

_____

_____

_____

_____

_____

_____

"It is good and pleasant when God's people live together in peace!"

Psalm 133:1

People I can turn to when I have a problem:

_____

_____

_____

_____

_____

_____

_____

_____

_____

In the future, I will try to handle tough times by

_____

_____

_____

_____

_____

_____

_____

_____

_____

_____

_____

_____

_____

_____

_____

_____

_____

_____

_____

_____

_____

_____

_____

Dealing with Conflict

A friend of mine said some mean things about my church. I prayed about it a long time, asking God to help me know what to do. I decided to write my friend a note, expressing my feelings about what she'd said. First, I told her that I still wanted to be her friend. I listed some of her good qualities and told her I appreciated her.

Then I wrote that I didn't think it was helpful to our friendship to criticize my church. I said, "It's important to our friendship to be gentle with each other about the things that are important to us. I know we can do it."

My friend called to apologize, we made up, and our friendship is going strong.

It's not always easy to face a situation like this, but it's easier when we ask God to help us do it with a loving spirit, and not in the heat of anger.

—Heather

It's a God Thing!

Write about a time you experienced conflict. What caused the conflict? What did you or the other person do to resolve it? What could have been done differently?

IT'S A GOD THING!
Helping Each Other in Tough Times

A boy in my school died suddenly. School seemed weird. It was quiet, except that kids and teachers were crying. One of my good friends was a friend of the boy. She called me and just cried over the phone. I tried to encourage her as best I could. At the funeral, I held my friend the whole time, not really knowing what to say.

A few months later, my grandmother died. My friend came to my house and we talked. It helped me, just having her there. It was the same situation as before, except that we had switched roles. Later, she wrote me the sweetest card that said, "God never meant for us to go through hard times alone. That's why we have each other."

I have kept her note, and I look at it whenever I'm down or disappointed or sad. It helps me remember I'm not alone, even in the tough times.

—Hayley

Conflict

I've seen people deal with conflicts in different ways. In this case, someone handled it well by

....
....
....
....
....
....
....
....
....
....
....
....
....
....
....
....
....
....
....
....
....
....
....
....
....

Challenge

I've faced challenges in the past. I overcame them by

....
....
....
....
....
....
....
....
....
....
....
....
....
....
....
....
....
....
....
....
....
....
....
....

Sometimes, it's a challenge to get along with someone. What I'm doing to try to get along with difficult people is

....
....
....
....
....
....
....
....
....
....
....
....
....
....
....
....
....
....
....
....
....
....
....
....
....
....
....
....
....
....

Struggle

Right now, I'm struggling with this difficult situation:

....
....
....
....
....
....
....
....
....
....
....
....
....
....
....
....
....
....
....
....
....
....
....
....

It's a God Thing!

Someone I know is facing a challenge. This is what they're going through:

....
....
....
....
....
....
....
....
....

I can help by

....
....
....
....
....
....
....
....

I learned a lot when I went through a tough situation. What I learned is

....
....
....
....
....
....

A GOD THING MOMENT
ABOUT TOUGH STUFF

(On this page, write about a God Thing that has happened to you.)

....
....
....
....
....
....
....
....
....
....
....
....
....
....
....
....
....
....
....
....
....
....
....
....
....
....
....
....
....
....

Everything's Changing

Chapter 7

DIVORCE

Troubles

LET
GO
OF . . .

Successes

PEER
PRESSURE

Moving

Decisions

Changing friends

NEW SCHOOL

Nothing Stays the Same!

A TV movie was being filmed in my town, and I signed up to be an "extra," along with about fifty other people. Our job was to act scared when the bad guys chased the good guy through the mall. When it was our turn to act, the director would yell, "Background!" and we would move around, crouching behind tables, acting as terrified as we could.

When I saw the movie, the "background" people were just a blurry bunch of unrecognizable bodies. (I'm pretty sure I saw my right arm!) The focus, of course, was on the star.

Do you ever feel like a "background" person? Like no one sees the real you? It happens to everyone, sooner or later. When it does, just try to be patient, learn what you can from being a "backgrounder," and know that someday your time in the forefront will come. *For real!*

—Karen

Make a list (on page 91) of all the changes you've experienced: family changes, lifestyle changes, people-in-your-life changes, body and health changes, relationship changes, changes in activities, likes and dislikes. Then write about whether these changes were good or bad, and what you learned from them.

They Say That . . .

I'm a butterfly in a cocoon,
a flower just waiting to bloom.
They say, "Just wait and see
how beautiful you'll be!"
And so they persist.
"Please stop!" I insist.
They smile and I groan,
"Please leave me alone!"
I'm not a bug in a rug
or a rose on a shrub.
I'll soon be grown
with a life of my own.
So don't pinch my cheeks
and tell me I'm sweet.
Just be there for me—
we'll get along, you'll see!

Write your own poem below.

_____

_____

_____

_____

_____

_____

_____

_____

_____

_____

_____

Passages, Paths, Puzzles

The biggest change I've experienced is

_____
_____
_____
_____
_____
_____
_____

It was tough because

_____
_____
_____
_____
_____
_____
_____
_____
_____
_____
_____
_____
_____
_____

THIS WAY

THAT WAY

ANOTHER WAY

It's a God Thing!

Someone who helped me get through the change was

_____

_____

by_____

_____

_____

_____

_____

_____

_____

_____

_____

"Life is like the weather: always changing. But, just as the sun, moon, and stars are constant, in our lives there is the constancy of hope, faith, and trust in the God who made us."

Karen Hill

I helped someone go through a time of change. Here's what happened:

_____

_____

_____

_____

_____

_____

_____

_____

_____

_____

_____

_____

_____

_____

_____

_____

_____

_____

_____

_____

_____

_____

_____

_____

_____

IT'S A GOD THING!
A Tug of War over Me

The last couple of years have been full of changes. First, my mom and dad decided to split up. My mom went to court to fight my dad for custody of me. Then she got married and we moved to a new town. New town, new house, new school, new stepdad! That was the hardest change of all—he was constantly saying mean things to me. So, after all the fighting, my mom let my dad take me. It made me feel like I was in the way; I wasn't sure if anybody really wanted me.

But near my dad's house is a nursing home. For some reason, I just stopped in one day and started visiting the people who lived there. I met a very sweet lady named Willie. She was so kind and always glad to see me. She was funny and smart and probably the wisest person I'll ever meet. I could tell her anything and she would listen and help me understand all the things that were happening. I love to write, and I could share my writing with her. She was always so interested.

The tug of war is still going on—now I'm back with my mom and things are pretty smooth, for the time being. I miss Willie, but I know that God placed her in my life at just the right time to help me get through the changing times.

—Alex

Change

The changes I'm going through right now:

....
....
....
....
....
....
....
....
....
....
....
....
....
....
....
....
....
....
....
....
....
....
....
....
....

Passages

When a change is happening, it's important to have someone to talk to. Someone I can really trust is

....
....
....
....
....
....
....

Not all changes are bad. Some good changes are

....
....
....
....
....
....
....
....
....
....
....
....

It's a God Thing!

In the past, I've experienced these changes. (They may have been where you live, a new school, new friends, or something else that changed in your life.)

Changes	Good	Bad	What I Learned
_____	___	___	_____
_____			_____
_____			_____
_____	___	___	_____
_____			_____
_____			_____
_____	___	___	_____
_____			_____
_____			_____
_____	___	___	_____
_____			_____
_____			_____
_____	___	___	_____
_____			_____
_____			_____

Experience

Some of my most exciting experiences include

....
....
....
....
....
....
....
....
....
....
....
....
....
....
....
....
....
....
....
....
....
....
....
....
....
....

It's a God Thing!

Some experiences that have helped me are

....
....
....
....
....
....
....
....
....
....
....
....
....
....
....
....
....
....
....
....
....
....
....
....
....
....
....
....
....
....

A GOD THING MOMENT
ABOUT CHANGES

(On this page, write about a God Thing that has happened to you.)

....
....
....
....
....
....
....
....
....
....
....
....
....
....
....
....
....
....
....
....
....
....
....
....
....
....
....
....
....
....

It's a God Thing!

School Stuff

For a change, grade yourself in these categories:

My Report Card

Name: _____

	A	B	C	D	F
Friendliness					
Treating People with Kindness					
Hope					
Honesty					
Joy					
Sense of Humor					
Patience					
Promptness					
Love of Others					
Helpfulness					
Doing My Best					
Being a Good Listener					
Showing Gratitude					

A-B-C 'Ya after Class!

School is much more than just books and tests. School is like a little city—a community where you do serious stuff and fun things, too. It's homework and friends and working in groups. It's successes and failures, ups and downs. It's quick lunches and early morning tutoring sessions, report cards and sports. Cheering the team and doing science experiments. Writing reports and hoping for extra credit!

For some teenagers, school and home are one and the same because they're homeschooled. Homeschoolers may not have to deal with lockers, gangs, and tardy bells, but they still face quizzes, term papers, and grades. Whether school is at home or at school, it can be fun, exciting, hard, and rewarding, all at once.

I go to school at _____ I'm in grade _____

My subjects are _____

_____

I really love learning about _____

My hardest subject is _____

I'm working on it by _____

_____

_____

_____

_____

It's a God Thing!

Fears at School

For some girls (and guys, too), the scary part of school isn't whether or not they're passing classes. It's whether or not they're *safe*. They hear too many news reports of too much violence at school. Coping with the stress of not feeling safe can add to all the other stresses of school.

In the space below, write about how safe you feel at school and whether safety is a concern to you: _____

_____

_____

_____

_____

_____

_____

These are the ways my school's principal, teachers, and other staff members have helped make my school a safe place:

_____

_____

_____

_____

_____

School Days

I ____like ____dislike school because

_____

_____

_____

_____

The best part of my day at school is

_____

_____

_____

Other schools I have attended:

_____

_____

> "Depend on the Lord. Trust him, and he will take care of you."
>
> **Psalm 37:5**

My best overall year at school was

_____

It was the best year because

_____

_____

_____

For high school, I'll go to

_____

_____

_____

School would be better if

_____

_____

_____

_____

_____

If I were principal for a day, I'd make these rules:

_____

_____

_____

_____

_____

_____

It's a God Thing!

God ___is ___isn't a big thing at my school. I think that's because

_____

_____

_____

_____

_____

_____

I can make God a bigger part of my school life by

_____

_____

_____

_____

_____

_____

_____

_____

_____

_____

_____

_____

_____

_____

_____

After school, my activities include

_____

_____

_____

_____

_____

_____

_____

_____

_____

_____

_____

_____

_____

_____

_____

School Stuff

99

IT'S A GOD THING!

Editor's Prayer

It was September. Mrs. Caskey, the newspaper sponsor at my school, was about to announce her choice for editor of the school paper. More than anything, I wanted to be chosen! But I felt that my best friend, Carmen, would get the job. She was a good writer and would be a great leader. I was afraid I'd be jealous if Carmen was chosen. And our friendship meant more to me than the honor.

I prayed hard about this. I asked God to help me be a good sport and to be supportive of Carmen. I specifically asked God to remove jealousy from my heart. When the announcement came, I felt very peaceful because I knew God would help me be happy for my friend. But then Mrs. Caskey called my name instead of Carmen's! I was surprised and excited, plus concerned about Carmen's feelings. But she was smiling and congratulating me—God had answered my prayer and had planted seeds of kindness in Carmen's heart as well. He did a God Thing and gave us both a God Moment! We had a great year working together on the paper.

—Karnie

In a similar situation, I would (did)

_____

_____

_____

_____

_____

Classes

My favorite classes:

....
....
....
....
....
....
....
....

My best subjects:

....
....
....
....
....
....
....
....
....
....
....
....

School Days

My favorite memory of school is

....

....

....

....

....

....

....

....

....

....

....

....

....

....

....

....

....

....

....

....

....

....

....

....

My worst memory of school is

....
....
....
....
....
....
....
....
....
....
....
....

The most embarrassing thing that ever happened to me at school was

....
....
....
....
....
....
....
....
....
....
....
....
....

Study

These are my study habits:

....
....
....
....
....
....
....
....
....
....
....
....

The best way I've found to study for tests:

....
....
....
....
....
....
....
....
....
....

In school, I've received these honors:

....
....
....
....
....
....
....
....
....
....
....
....
....
....
....
....
....
....
....
....
....
....
....
....
....
....
....
....
....

A GOD THING MOMENT ABOUT SCHOOL

(On this page, write about a God Thing that has happened to you about school.)

....
....
....
....
....
....
....
....
....
....
....
....
....
....
....
....
....
....
....
....
....
....
....
....
....

It's a God Thing!

Can a Christian Be Cool?

Chapter 9

Draw a cross, then write in it the names of some "cool" Christians you know.

Following Jesus:
A Win-Win Decision

How do you define "coolness"? According to the *Teens' Contemporary Language Dictionary*,[1] coolness is the opposite of "geekiness." A cool person doesn't bail when people make fun of God or take his name in vain. A cool person is more concerned with her relationship with God than with making an impression on people. If you're working through this journal, you're definitely cool!

A "cool" Christian is someone who

_____

_____

_____

Someone I know who is really cool:

_____

This is what makes her (him) cool:

_____

_____

_____

_____

_____

[1] Otherwise known as a list of current teen jargon compiled by my teenage buds.

It's a God Thing!

Standing Up for God

I'm always getting e-mails that say, "If you believe in Jesus, then you should pass this on." That might be a good thing to do, but God doesn't need you to pass along an e-mail to show your love for him. If someone's encouraging you to do something you know is wrong, and you find the courage to say "no," then that's one way of standing up for God. Or saying a prayer during the "moment of silence" at school—that's another way of standing up for God. It means that you know who you are, and your faith is going to keep you strong, and you won't let anything or anybody talk you out of it.

—Noel

Christians Can Be Heroes

I can be a cool Christian when I'm involved in

_____

_____

_____

_____

_____

Ways that Christians can have fun:

_____

_____

_____

_____

_____

_____

_____

_____

_____

_____

Other opportunities to show my "coolness" include:

_____

_____

_____

_____

_____

_____

_____

_____

_____

_____

My Hero:

Honors God

Encourages others

Recognizes her or his gifts

Overcomes obstacles

It's a God Thing!

A Christian hero I personally know is

_____
_____
_____
_____

This person is my hero because

_____
_____
_____
_____
_____
_____
_____
_____
_____

Other heroes in my life include

_____
_____
_____
_____
_____
_____
_____
_____
_____

I want to be a hero in the life of

_____
_____
_____
_____
_____
_____
_____

Some of my qualities that will make me a hero:

_____
_____
_____
_____
_____
_____
_____

"We have many people of faith around us. Their lives tell us what faith means."

Hebrews 12:1

Can a Christian Be Cool?

IT'S A GOD THING!

Not Alone

I had to go to school early one morning to make up a test. I passed by a few classrooms where teachers were getting ready for the day. Then I came to Room 217. I noticed seven or eight teachers sitting at the students' desks. The teachers all seemed to be looking down, and their hands were folded in their laps or on the desks. One teacher was standing up, and he was looking down, too. I thought, *That's kinda weird—wonder what's going on?*

Then I heard one of the teachers say, "Also, Lord, we ask that you . . ." I couldn't hear the rest, but that was all I needed. They were praying. At 8 A.M. in a public school, a handful of teachers were praying (probably about us kids!). Wow! I was excited to discover this group of teachers who weren't afraid to

demonstrate their faith. Knowing they were there really gave me courage, and it made me feel that I'm not alone—there's definitely a cool bunch of Christian teachers at my school!

—Jennifer

Coolness

The coolest Christian I know is

....

because

....
....
....
....
....
....
....
....
....
....
....
....
....
....
....
....
....
....
....
....
....
....

Heroes

A hero is someone who has these traits:

....
....
....
....
....
....

To me, a hero is someone who

....
....
....
....
....
....
....

I once felt like a hero because

....
....
....
....
....
....
....

Write an imaginary letter to your hero:

Faith

My pledge of faith:

....
....
....
....
....
....
....
....
....
....
....
....
....
....
....
....
....
....
....
....
....
....
....
....
....
....
....

How I came to know about Jesus:

....
....
....
....
....
....
....
....
....
....
....
....
....
....
....
....
....
....
....
....
....
....
....
....
....
....
....
....
....
....

A GOD THING MOMENT ABOUT BEING A COOL CHRISTIAN

(On this page, write about a God Thing that has
happened to you because you are a cool Christian.)

....

....

....

....

....

....

....

....

....

....

....

....

....

....

....

....

....

....

....

....

....

....

....

....

....

Wanted:
The Perfect Guy

Must have these qualities:

1.

2.

3.

4.

5.

Figuring Them Out!

There are basically two types of guys:

Boyfriends

(The ones you think about, the ones you have imaginary conversations with, the ones you imagine sending you flowers every day and telling you how gorgeous you are.)

Friend-boys

(Those great guys who are your "buds"—whom you can confide in, as if they were your brothers.)

Some people say guys and girls can't be friends, that it always goes back to "romance." But I think it's great to have guy friends. Just as in any relationship, the basics are honesty, caring, and consideration. Friend-boys can be awesome friends.

I have (don't have) a boyfriend: _____

I have (don't have) a "friend-boy": _____

The perfect guy would be like this: _____

_____

_____

_____

_____

It's a God Thing!

Guys Are Confusing!

Guys are so many things: they're sweet and caring, sometimes they're weird—they're really confusing! (And they think *we're* confusing.) Some guys have a macho, cool attitude, always trying to impress every girl in sight, or they can be just the opposite. I think you should pick boyfriends the same way you choose your girlfriends—on the basis of who they are and what kind of people they are, rather than how cute they are or how they dress.

—Kara

THANK YOU!

Before you get a huge crush on a guy, think about this:

How does he treat other people? (Is he kind?) • Is he hung up on how great he thinks he is? • Is he involved in things I want to avoid? • Is he respectful to girls? • Does he show off? • Does he brag? • What's his home life like? • Is he serious about school or does he just blow it off? • Does he hang out with the wrong kind of guys (do drugs, etc.)? • What's his relationship with God? • And remember, having a boyfriend isn't the most important thing in the world!

About Guys

The coolest guy at school (or church) is

_____

_____

The girls think he's awesome because

_____

_____

_____

_____

I'm attracted to this kind of guy (jock, studious, class clown, etc.):

_____

_____

_____

_____

The kind of guy God would want me to choose is

_____

_____

_____

_____

_____

_____

I flirt ___a lot ___a little ___sometimes ___it depends on the guy!

If I liked a guy and my best friend thought he wasn't good for me, I'd

_____

_____

_____

_____

_____

_____

_____

_____

My parents have rules about guys. Their rules are:

_____

_____

_____

_____

_____

_____

_____

_____

___I think the rules stink. ___I respect the rules.

How Do I Act Around Boys?

I used to act different around guys. I would try to change my personality (laugh louder, etc.) just to get guys to like me. But then I realized that if a guy liked me, he should like ME, not the me I was pretending to be. I also remembered that God made me the way I am—he loves me the way I am, and so do my friends and family. This is important! I don't want to change myself for a guy!

—Andrea

The me I want guys to see is

_____

_____

_____

I'm fun because

_____

_____

_____

_____

My ideal relationship with a guy would be like this:

_____

_____

_____

_____

Sidewalk Survey: What Do Girls Say about PDA*—Is It Cool or Uncool?

"It's definitely not cool. It's gross."
—Abby, 12

"I think handholding, hugging, and little kisses are okay, but I don't like it when people make out in public."
—Shelly, 14

"Sweet, romantic gestures are all right."
—Victoria, 14

"There's a time and a place for everything—and it's sure not in front of school at 8 a.m.!"
—Suzanne, 13

*Public Display of Affection, aka kissing and stuff

Wrong Place, Wrong Time, Wrong Guy!

I'm not old enough to date yet (at least that's my parents' rule), but I was determined to break the rule when Chad (the absolute coolest guy at school and starting quarterback for our team) asked me out. The plan was for us to meet at the movies (my parents would think I was at a girlfriend's) and then he and I would take off in his older brother's car. (I didn't even worry about the fact that he didn't have a license!)

That night, as I waited for him, I started feeling nervous. Not only was I about to disobey my parents, I had just lied to them—big time. When Chad got there, he looked different. He was talking loud and acting weird. And he'd been drinking.

Something told me: "Don't get into the car with this guy!" When I refused to go, he got mad, got into the car, and raced out of the parking lot. I called my parents.

The next day, I learned Chad had been charged with drunk driving. He was kicked off the team and suspended from school. When I heard the news, I knew God had been watching over me that night, protecting me from a dangerous situation.

—Mamie

PDA
Public Display of Affection

Stories I've heard about PDA:

....
....
....
....
....
....
....
....
....
....
....
....
....

What I think about PDA:

....
....
....
....
....
....
....
....
....
....
....
....
....
....
....
....
....

Purity

About staying pure until marriage, I think

My pledge of purity:

....
....
....
....
....
....
....
....
....

How I plan to keep my promise:

....
....
....
....
....
....
....
....
....
....
....
....
....
....
....
....
....

Romance

My favorite romantic stories:

....
....
....
....
....
....
....
....
....
....

Romantic things a guy could do for me:

....
....
....
....
....
....
....

Romantic things a I could do for a guy:

....
....
....
....
....
....
....

Friend-boys

My "friend-boys" are true friends. Here's how I know for sure:

....
....
....
....
....
....
....
....
....
....
....
....
....
....
....
....

My friend-boys and I do these things together:

....
....
....
....
....
....
....
....
....
....
....

A GOD THING MOMENT
ABOUT GUYS

(On this page, write about a God Thing that has happened to you.)

....
....
....
....
....
....
....
....
....
....
....
....
....
....
....
....
....
....
....
....
....
....
....
....
....
....
....

It's a God Thing!

When Life Hurts

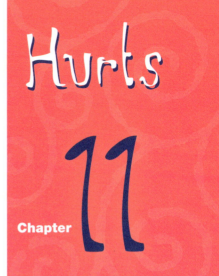

Chapter 11

Put your tears in this box.

Living through Sad Times

Wouldn't it be nice if life didn't hurt so much at times? If people we love didn't experience pain or have to die . . . if families weren't broken apart by divorce . . . if children didn't have to go hungry . . . if we all felt safe, all the time? Of course, the reality is that life—as great as it can be, as full of joy as it can be—also includes pain. None of us completely escape it. For non-Christians, this is really bad news. But for those who know Jesus, our painful times are softened by knowing that God is with us, always. He really, really loves us and cares about our tears and sorrows and fears. No matter how hard life can be, God never leaves us. When we don't understand the "whys" of life, we can trust our heavenly Father to help us get through to the "joys" of life.

The most painful time of my life was when

_____

_____

_____

When I think about it, I feel

_____

_____

_____

Walking through Dark Days

Here are some gentle ways to help your hurting heart:

* Don't expect too much of yourself. Give yourself time to grieve or to work through the sadness or problem you're experiencing.

* Allow yourself to walk through the experience in your own way. There are no rules for dealing with pain.

* Find someone you can confide in and talk to.

* Look for your own personal key to calmness. Restoring the peace and joy to your spirit may be accomplished in many different ways—each person has a different "key." It might be listening to special music or going to a quiet place or being in the midst of nature. It could be reading favorite inspirational books or Scriptures or poems. Perhaps it's writing in your journal or doing something for someone else.

Will It Always Hurt This Much?

One of the hardest times I went through was

_____
_____
_____
_____
_____
_____
_____
_____
_____
_____

This is how I felt:

_____
_____
_____
_____
_____
_____
_____
_____
_____

Someone who helped me get through it was

_____
_____
_____
_____
_____
_____
_____

He/she helped me by

_____
_____
_____
_____
_____
_____
_____
_____

"I can do all things through Christ because he gives me strength."

Philippians 4:13

It's a God Thing!

"Sad experiences are like dark tunnels. But remember that the light at the end of that tunnel is God, and he will bring you through the darkness. Let prayer guide you through."

Pam

My thoughts on dealing with emotional pain:

_____
_____
_____
_____
_____
_____
_____
_____
_____
_____
_____
_____

What I learned from the pain was

_____
_____
_____
_____
_____
_____

These kinds of things cause me pain:

_____
_____
_____
_____
_____
_____
_____
_____

Someday We'll Be Together

My little brother, Carlos, was so special, always happy. He was only three years old when he was diagnosed with cancer. My parents and sisters and I were sad, but not all of the time. Carlos's health would improve for a while and we would all be very excited and happy. But soon he would become sick again. Each time this happened, he got weaker. It hurt me to see him in the hospital, on the verge of death. But even then, he would smile and show us his happy nature.

When Carlos died, our whole family was in the room with him. My mom wept as she held him in her arms. I cannot tell you what a sad day it was. But even through my sadness, something inside of me felt peaceful. It was because I knew my sweet little brother was in heaven with Jesus. When I share this story, I tell it with great joy and happiness, knowing that someday we will all be together, forever.

—Lina

Tears

Sometimes it helps to express all the questions you have about sadness. Write them on this page, along with your fears, anger, and disappointments:

....

....

....

....

....

....

....

....

....

....

....

....

....

....

....

....

....

....

....

....

....

....

....

....

....

....

Sadness

The sad times I've seen people experience, and what I've learned from them:

....

....

....

....

....

....

....

....

....

....

....

This is how I try to deal with sad situations:

....

....

....

....

....

....

....

....

....

....

....

....

Pain

Once, I caused pain for someone else. Here's what happened:

....
....
....
....
....
....
....
....
....

A painful situation that could have been avoided was

....
....
....
....
....
....
....
....
....
....
....
....

My thoughts on dealing with emotional pain:

....
....
....
....
....
....
....
....
....
....

Hope

The other side of sadness is hope. Here are the reasons
I have hope:

....
....
....
....
....
....
....
....
....
....
....
....
....
....
....
....
....
....
....
....
....
....
....
....
....
....

Here are the joys that are part of my life:

....
....
....
....
....
....
....
....
....
....
....
....
....
....
....
....
....
....
....
....
....
....
....
....
....
....
....
....
....
....
....

A GOD THING MOMENT ABOUT SADNESS

(On this page, write about a God Thing that has happened to you.)

....
....
....
....
....
....
....
....
....
....
....
....
....
....
....
....
....
....
....
....
....
....
....
....
....
....
....

Me, the athlete

Chapter 12

Glue, paste, or tape down some pictures of athletes you admire.

My Sportin' Life!

The words that warm the heart of sports-minded girls like me: *swim, dive, race, hoops, bats, balls, tennis, soccer, track, work out, pump up, train, score, home run, goal!* And don't forget *sweat, medals, teams, scores,* and *sneakers!* Perfume and makeup are fine. Music is great. Guys are okay. But sports have captured my heart!

My favorite sport is_____

I'm best at_____

I like to watch _____

Playing sports is a great . . .

Discipline

aerobics

Teamwork

Energy!

On God's Team

Sports are fun, challenging, and provide a whole new way to express ourselves. We can learn a lot from athletics: the importance of teamwork, getting along with others, and showing respect for each other. But you don't have to be an athlete only in sports— you can also be an athlete for God. He's the head coach! If you're on his team, then you can play the game of life for the joy of the Lord and always win!

—Andrea

Me, the Athlete

145

Winners in the Game of Life

Sports are important in my life in this way:

_____

_____

_____

_____

_____

_____

> "I want to become a famous athlete and have people ask me how I do it, so I can respond, 'God gave me the talent.'"
>
> **Alisha**

My favorite pro athlete is

_____

_____

My favorite pro team is

_____

_____

If I could meet anyone in sports, it would be

_____

_____

If I could go to any championship event, it would be

_____

_____

_____

_____

_____

_____

The best coach I ever had was

_____

_____

_____

He (she) was a great coach because

_____

_____

_____

_____

_____

_____

_____

_____

_____

_____

It's a God Thing!

The best team I played on was

_____

_____

It was the best team because

_____

_____

_____

_____

_____

_____

_____

Friends I've made through sports:

_____

_____

_____

_____

_____

_____

_____

Write about how the discipline of sports
affects your everyday life:

_____

_____

_____

_____

_____

_____

The Girl with the Hustle

I love playing sports!! I love watching sports, too, but I'd rather be playing. It's the most fun thing I do. I'm on the basketball team, but I also want to learn boxing and soccer. My goal is to go to college on a basketball scholarship. Off the court, I'm kind of quiet and a little bit shy, but in the game, I turn into a "hustle monster"! Being aggressive is a good quality in an athlete, but when the game is over, I leave that quality in the gym and turn into quiet me again.

—Noel

IT'S A GOD THING!
A Real Champion

As an athlete, I hear the same message over and over: "Win! Win! Win!" Some of my coaches have stressed good sportsmanship. So I've wondered: *How can I accomplish both? How can I be a tough competitor and demonstrate Christian kindness and sportsmanship at the same time?* I came across a story of an athlete who seemed to understand how to be a good sport *and* a champion. Her name is Esther Kim. Esther had a dream: to win a spot on the U.S. Olympic tae kwon do team. Her chances were better than most; she had spent years preparing for the competition and was the strongest contender to win. But Esther didn't make it to the Olympics. At the national level, she was scheduled to compete against her best friend, Kay. Just before the event, Kay injured her knee. Esther knew the victory was hers, because her friend couldn't possibly win with an injured knee.

So, with victory in sight, Esther did something incredible—she gave up her spot on the team, allowing her best friend to take her place. Esther said that what she did made her feel like a champion for the first time in her life. Her dad (who was the girls' coach) saw the outcome as a God Thing, saying that God helped both girls become champions. Esther Kim's story helped me understand how to win in the game of life.

— Lisa

It's a God Thing!

Sports

My history in athletics:

....
....
....
....
....
....
....
....
....
....
....
....
....
....
....
....
....
....
....
....
....
....
....
....
....
....
....

Team

Some teams I've played on and the friends I've made:

....
....
....
....
....
....
....
....
....

If I had my own "Dream Team," the sport would be

....

This is who I'd want on the team:

....
....
....
....
....
....
....
....

The coach would be

....
....

Sports Goals

My plans, goals, and schedules for the years ahead in sports:

....
....
....
....
....
....
....
....
....
....
....
....
....
....
....
....
....
....
....
....
....
....
....
....
....
....
....

Compete

The hardest teams we've played:

....
....
....
....
....
....
....
....
....
....
....
....
....
....
....
....
....
....
....
....
....
....
....
....

It's a God Thing!

Sportsmanship

My experience with good (or bad) sportsmanship:

....
....
....
....
....
....
....
....
....
....
....
....
....
....
....

Through sports, I've learned these life lessons:

....
....
....
....
....
....
....
....
....
....

A GOD THING MOMENT
IN SPORTS

(On this page, write about a God Thing that has happened to you.)

....
....
....
....
....
....
....
....
....
....
....
....
....
....
....
....
....
....
....
....
....
....
....
....
....
....
....

God and Me

Chapter 13

Write down one of your favorite prayers here.

_____

_____

_____

_____

_____

_____

_____

_____

_____

_____

_____

_____

_____

_____

_____

_____

_____

God: Priority #1

No matter who we are, where we live, whether we're rich or poor, cool or geeky, superachievers or underwhelmers, there is a God in heaven who delights in us. We are his, and he loves us, despite our mistakes and flaws. What a great thought! In our busy, hectic lives, spending time with him can refresh our spirits like a "Big Gulp" on a hot summer day. Suggestion: Try to find some time every day to spend with your heavenly Father. Take a "Big Gulp" of his love!

This is what God means to me:

_____

_____

_____

_____

_____

_____

_____

_____

_____

_____

_____

It's a God Thing!

My Quiet Place

There's a place I go . . .
I meet God there.
It's a quiet place,
for just us two.
And when we're together,
all the world fades away.
It's just God and me.
Together, we can face anything.
I share with him my mistakes,
my cares, my fears, my hopes.
He listens, I listen—
in the perfect, quiet place in my heart
where he lives with me.

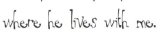

Walking with God

When I was a kid, I thought God was like this:

_____

_____

_____

Now that I'm older, I see him this way:

_____

_____

_____

_____

"Don't worry, because I am with you. Don't be afraid, because I am your God. I will make you strong and will help you. I will support you with my right hand that saves you."

Isaiah 41:10

I'm grateful to God for these blessings:

_____

_____

_____

_____

_____

_____

_____

I have these questions for God:

_____

_____

_____

_____

_____

The best gift I could give God would be

_____

_____

_____

_____

_____

I find it ___easy ___hard to tell others about God because

_____

_____

_____

My favorite time to pray is

_____

I'd like to spend more time with God each day. Here's how and when I can start doing this:

_____

_____

_____

_____

It's a God Thing!

When I want to praise God, I like to sing

_____

_____

_____

My special place for spending time
alone with God is

_____

_____

_____

If I had a whole day to spend alone with
God, this is where I'd go and what I'd do:

_____

_____

_____

_____

_____

"I am guiding you in wisdom. And
I am leading you to do what is
right. Nothing will hold you back.
You will not be overwhelmed."

Proverbs 4:11–12

_____

_____

_____

_____

_____

_____

_____

My ☆ Prayers

Knowing and loving God has made it much easier to overcome peer
pressure, which is a major daily struggle! I used to be tempted
to say cuss words, but I've been praying about it, and those prayers have really helped
me. I pray every night when I go to bed (this is my "quiet place"). I ask God's help with
peer pressure, judging others, making decisions, and controlling what I say. He makes me
feel stronger in all these areas. It's because of prayer.

—Pamela

IT'S A GOD THING!

Discovering God

During the worst time of my life, I found God. My family didn't go to church, read the Bible, pray, or even talk about God. I didn't know anything about Jesus or what he did for us. But when my parents were getting a divorce, God sort of walked into the middle of that whole awful time and introduced himself to me.

The way it happened was pretty simple, really. My friend Lindsey invited me to go to church with her. That may not seem like a big deal, but it sure was for me. I heard for the first time about a God who loves me all the time, regardless of circumstances, a God who sent his own Son to Earth in order to save me. Getting to know God also brought me in touch with a whole church full of people who were living their lives to please him.

Even though I was losing my earthly family, I was gaining a heavenly Father and a spiritual family. I think God's timing was perfect.

—Amy

It's a God Thing!

Heart

I know God lives in my heart because

....
....
....
....
....
....
....
....
....
....
....
....
....
....
....
....
....
....
....
....
....
....
....
....
....
....
....
....

Prayer

My prayer life:

....
....
....
....
....
....
....
....

When I pray, I talk to God about

....
....
....
....
....
....
....
....
....
....
....
....
....

My special prayer to God:

....
....
....
....
....
....
....
....
....
....
....
....
....
....
....
....
....
....

Some things that only God knows about me:

....
....
....
....
....
....
....
....
....
....
....
....
....

Faith

People who have helped my faith grow, and how:

....
....
....
....
....
....
....
....
....
....
....
....

My favorite Bible character is

....
....

This is what I've learned from his (her) story:

....
....
....
....
....
....

Some things I have come to understand about my heavenly Father:

....
....
....
....
....
....
....
....
....
....
....
....
....
....
....
....
....
....
....
....
....
....
....
....
....
....
....

A GOD THING MOMENT ABOUT MY HEAVENLY FATHER

(On this page, write about a God Thing that has happened to you.)

....
....
....
....
....
....
....
....
....
....
....
....
....
....
....
....
....
....
....
....
....
....
....
....
....

Money Tales

Make tracings of a quarter on this page. Within the circles, write down the things you would like to do with the money you earn.

Dollars and Sense

Saving, spending, buying, lending, adding, subtracting, earning, splurging: the tale of the pocketbook. Even though people say money doesn't matter, it is a fact of life. Whether you have a lot or a little of the green stuff, managing it wisely is a godly thing to do. Since everything we have comes from God, he expects us to handle money wisely, while not making it the most important factor in our lives. For those who are blessed financially, the challenge to share with those less fortunate is even greater. Money is a tool with which we can help and serve others in our world.

My family's financial circumstances are

_____

_____

My spending money comes from

_____

_____

When I want more money for something special, I

_____

_____

I can talk easily to my parents about money. ___Yes ___No

Talk about money causes stress in my home. ___Yes ___No

It's a God Thing!

Fun for Free

Sure, a lot of things cost money, but there's a ton of fun to be had for free. You don't have to be rich to enjoy life! There are free events and sites in every town. For example, in our town we have several free parks where you can have cook-outs, play sand volleyball, even take a boom box and dance. There's a soda bottling plant that offers free tours. (They give you free sodas!)

You can even create the fun things to do. Have a video scavenger hunt in your neighbor-hood. Have a makeup party—invite your friends to a sleepover and help make each other up, do crazy hair things, etc. Be imaginative— you can think of a zillion ways to have a blast without spending a lot of cash!

"Everyone who has been given much will be responsible for much. Much more will be expected from the one who has been given more."

Luke 12:48

Piggy Banks and Spending Sprees

"Give this command to those who are rich with things of this world. Tell them not to be proud. Tell them to hope in God, not their money. Money cannot be trusted, but God takes care of us richly. He gives us everything to enjoy. Tell the rich people to do good and to be rich in doing good deeds. Tell them to be happy to give and ready to share."

1 Timothy 6:17–18

____I have a hard time saving money because_____

_____

_____

I'm saving up for

_____

_____

_____

I spend most of my money on

_____

_____

_____

___I love to shop.

___I couldn't care less about shopping.

___When I go to the mall, I run out of money too soon.

___My parents give me a $_____ allowance ___weekly ___monthly.

I ___earn my allowance or ___can make extra money by doing these chores:

_____

_____

_____

I earn extra money in these ways:

_____

_____

_____

_____

____I'm good at saving money because_____

_____

_____

_____

This is what I think about doing chores for my family:

_____

_____

_____

I have a _____positive _____negative attitude about my chores. To do better in this area, I could

_____

_____

_____

_____

_____

_____

How do you manage your money? Does anyone try to control how you save and spend, or do you have complete control?

_____

_____

_____

_____

_____

_____

_____

Some ways I can help those in need:

_____

_____

_____

_____

_____

_____

_____

_____

Giving to Others

Just as there will always be people around you who have more money, there will always be people in need. God expects us to share with those in need, whether it's money, time, or service. There's no greater blessing than knowing you are sharing your gifts with others.

"Do not owe people anything."

Romans 13:8

IT'S A GOD THING!
My Favorite Vacation

My family was planning a dream vacation: a week on a beautiful beach. To make it possible, everybody (Mom, Dad, my brother, and I) started saving. We labeled an empty coffee can "Beach Bucks." We chipped in allowances and money earned from baby-sitting and mowing yards. Mom tried to spend less at the grocery store. Dad worked extra hours at his job.

Then our friends the Simonsens lost their home in a fire and one of their children was badly burned. That night I said, "I've been thinking about the Simonsens." Dad said, "I've been thinking about them, too." We all knew what we needed to do. We couldn't enjoy the beach when our friends were in such need. We gave them our vacation money.

When summer came, we packed up as planned and piled into the car. Dad drove around for a while and then took us home. We spent the week at home, pretending it was the beach. We spread out our beach towels on the living room floor, watched beach movies, and ate hot dogs. We read books and played games together.

We didn't exactly have our "dream vacation" that summer, but we experienced something even better: knowing that our financial blessings were used to help some of God's people.

—Hannah

Cash

I can better manage my money by

....
....
....
....
....
....
....
....
....
....
....
....
....
....
....
....
....
....
....
....
....
....
....
....
....
....
....

Saving

How I've saved money, where it came from, and how I will use it:

....
....
....
....
....
....
....
....
....
....
....
....
....
....
....
....
....
....
....
....
....
....
....
....

Advice I have received about how to manage my money:

....
....
....
....
....
....
....
....
....
....
....
....
....
....
....
....
....
....
....
....
....
....
....
....
....
....
....
....
....

Giving

I want to help others with my money and time. Here's how I've helped in the past and how I'd like to help in the future:

....
....
....
....
....
....
....
....
....
....
....
....
....
....
....
....
....
....
....
....
....
....

How to locate people whom I could help (church office, volunteer agency, hospitals, nursing homes, neighborhood, etc.):

....
....
....
....
....
....
....
....
....
....
....
....
....
....
....

These are some things my family has done to share our gifts:

....
....
....
....
....
....
....
....
....
....

A GOD THING MOMENT
ABOUT MONEY

(On this page, write about a God Thing that has happened to you.)

....

....

....

....

....

....

....

....

....

....

....

....

....

....

....

....

....

....

....

....

....

....

....

....

....

....

....

It's a God Thing!

Expressing Myself

Design your own billboard to describe yourself, pasting or taping below words clipped from magazines.

Delightfully Different

Wouldn't the world be boring if we were all just alike? We would all be like a bunch of robots from the planet Dullsville! How could we tell each other apart? Wasn't it a cool God Thing to make each of us different and special? Finding the uniqueness in ourselves can be a great adventure. The wonder, the discoveries about ourselves can continue for a lifetime. Use this chapter to explore the adventure with your name on it!

Some things that make me unique:

_____

_____

_____

_____

My life is special because

_____

_____

_____

_____

_____

_____

_____

_____

_____

_____

It's a God Thing!

Who's Me?

I answer to Katie or Kiki
Or Kay, and sometimes Kate,
But who's the real me?
And what path will I take?
I know I like shopping
And playing b-ball,
But surely there's more—
That couldn't be all!
I can sing all day
Or sleep till noon,
Make good grades,
Bake brownies, too.
It's there, can you see?
That big question mark—
It lives deep within me,
There—inside my heart.
It asks, Who am I?
What will I be?
I wonder, oh my,
Who's the real me?

—Caitlin

The Me I See

In my life, I have felt

____happy

____sad

____silly

____lonely

____blessed

____mischievous

____angry

____nervous

____excited

____irritated

____confused

"Live creatively, friends. . . . Make a careful exploration of who you are and the work you have been given, and then sink yourself into that. . . . Each of you must take responsibility for doing the creative best you can with your own life."

Galatians 6:1, 4–5
(The Message)

Write about one of these emotions, and an experience that you had in dealing with it:

_____

_____

_____

_____

_____

_____

_____

_____

_____

_____

_____

_____

_____

_____

_____

It's a God Thing!

This is my personal energy source:

_____
_____
_____
_____
_____
_____
_____
_____
_____
_____
_____
_____
_____
_____
_____
_____
_____
_____

I get really excited about

_____
_____
_____

because _____

_____
_____
_____
_____
_____
_____

IT'S A GOD THING!

Going the Distance

Last summer I went on a backpacking trip—our goal was to climb a mountain in Colorado. I was really nervous about going. I was scared, and doubted myself. Would I be able to make it to the top of the mountain? Would I freak out when it was my turn to rappel down the cliff on a rope? I don't remember a time when I had so many questions about myself. The real question was, "What am I made of? Do I have the inner toughness to get through this?"

Our first challenge was to hike to the campsite. I got very tired, but knew I had to keep going. Before I knew it, steps had turned into yards, and yards had turned into miles, and miles had turned into our destination. That night at the campfire, one of the guides asked me how I liked it. My answer was, "It was the hardest thing I've ever done." I told him I would never go again. But by the end of the week, I could look back and see how far I'd come, and what I'd endured to accomplish the goal. I was proud of myself! I realized if you don't push yourself to reach your goals, you will never know what you're really capable of achieving.

—Caroline

Career

My career plan:

....
....
....
....
....
....
....
....
....
....
....
....
....
....
....
....
....
....
....
....
....
....
....
....
....
....
....

Journey

Life is like a journey. Right now, I'm traveling the road called

....

These are some of the sights along the way:

....

....

....

....

....

....

....

....

....

....

....

....

....

....

....

....

....

....

This is how I see the road ahead:

....
....
....
....
....
....
....
....
....
....
....
....
....
....
....
....
....
....
....
....
....
....
....
....
....
....
....

Future

I'm excited about the future because

....
....
....
....
....
....
....
....
....
....
....
....
....
....
....
....
....
....
....
....
....
....
....
....

This is how I would describe my personal adventure:

....
....
....
....
....
....
....
....
....
....
....
....
....
....
....
....
....
....
....
....
....
....
....
....
....
....
....
....
....
....
....
....

A GOD THING MOMENT ABOUT ME

I know God has a plan for each of us. Though I may not know for a long time to come, I'm beginning to understand what he has in store for me. This is what I think God wants me to do with my life:

....
....
....
....
....
....
....
....
....
....
....
....
....
....
....
....
....
....
....
....
....
....
....
....
....

It's a God Thing!

Write a letter to yourself from your heavenly Father, reminding yourself of how much he loves you and why you're special to him.

Dear _____,

_____

_____

_____

_____

_____

_____

_____

_____

_____

_____

_____

_____

_____

_____

_____

_____

_____

_____

_____

_____

_____

_____

_____

Love,
Your heavenly Father

IT'S A GOD THING!

You've come to the end of your journal, but your *journey* is just beginning! In the days, months, and years ahead, you'll be reaching some of the goals you wrote about. You'll be conquering some of the fears you journaled. You'll meet new friends (and maybe even that guy you wrote about). There's a great adventure of living ahead of you!

I hope you'll keep writing about some of the "God Things" that happen in your life. Think about relationships, changes in your life, ways you've come to understand God better. Think about God Things in the lives of those around you. Your record of God Things will become a prayer of thanksgiving for God's hand in your life. And keep watching for God Things! They happen when you least expect them!

Thanks for letting me tag along on your adventure. See ya in the next book!

Your "bud,"

Karen Hill

P.S. Do you have an "It's a God Thing!" story you'd like to share? Send it to me at:

Tommy Nelson
P.O. Box 141000
Nashville, TN 37214

Or email me at:
prdept@tommynelson.com